Author **Thomas Emson's** acclaimed **HOW TO WRITE A NOVEL IN 6 MONTHS** has received widespread praise as a no-nonsense, easy-to-follow, sure-fire way to achieve your dream of writing a novel.

The accompanying **Workbook** also provides aspiring authors with the tools necessary to reach their goals.

And now use this **Notebook** to gather ideas, sketch out scenes, create characters, write that First Draft, and take your first steps to being a published writer.

Please return this notebook to

....

....

....

....

Thank you

Printed in Great Britain
by Amazon

59875924R00088